T0366283

This book belongs to:

_____

Presented by:

_____

On:

_____

FROM THE AUTHOR OF

In the Midst of a Turbulent Sea.

Answering *and* Understanding *the* CALL OF GOD *for* Your Life.

WORKBOOK

CHINYERE NWAKWUE

iUniverse, Inc.
Bloomington

Answering and Understanding the CALL of God for Your Life workbook

Copyright © 2013 Chinyere Nwakwue

All rights reserved. No part of this book may be used or reproduced by any means, graphic, electronic, or mechanical, including photocopying, recording, taping or by any information storage retrieval system without the written permission of the publisher except in the case of brief quotations embodied in critical articles and reviews.

All scripture quotations are taken from the King James Version of the Holy Bible

iUniverse books may be ordered through booksellers or by contacting:

iUniverse
1663 Liberty Drive
Bloomington, IN 47403
www.iuniverse.com
1-800-Authors (1-800-288-4677)

Because of the dynamic nature of the Internet, any Web addresses or links contained in this book may have changed since publication and may no longer be valid. The views expressed in this work are solely those of the author and do not necessarily reflect the views of the publisher, and the publisher hereby disclaims any responsibility for them.

Any people depicted in stock imagery provided by Thinkstock are models, and such images are being used for illustrative purposes only.

Certain stock imagery © Thinkstock.

ISBN: 9781-4759-6122-5 (sc)
ISBN: 978-1-4759-6123-2 (e)

Library of Congress Control Number: 2012921697

Printed in the United States of America

iUniverse rev. date: 3/15/2013

"Study to shew thyself approved unto God, a workman that needeth not to be ashamed, rightly dividing the word of truth" (2 Timothy 2:15).

"Thy word is a lamp unto my feet, and a light unto my path" (Psalm 119:105).

"All scripture is given by inspiration of God, and is profitable for doctrine, for reproof, for correction, for instruction in righteousness: That the man of God may be perfect, throughly furnished unto all good works" (2 Timothy 3:16–17).

Answering and Understanding the CALL of God for Your Life Workbook is designed to help these categories of individuals reach their destiny in Christ. To help those yearning to answer the call of God; to help those already in the ministry understand the depth of the call of God in their lives—buckle up and tighten their loose belts in all areas. Furthermore, to help those with questions about calling and ministry in general receive the grace of God and encouragement to press forward. Finally, to bring light to those who are struggling with the call of God and ministry at large. If you find yourself in any of these categories, praise Jesus, this book is right for you.

Answering and Understanding the call of God can be confusing and challenging, however, having a full knowledge of your position in Christ brings you a step closer to that level God wants you to be. Most importantly allowing the Holy Spirit to take full preeminence in your life will lead you to your destiny in Christ. This workbook will walk you through step-by-step as you dig deeper into the word of God extensively to tap from his eternal wisdom to accomplish his will and purpose for your life. May the Almighty God grant you understanding as you dedicate your life and time to study this workbook in Jesus' name. Amen.

A broad and comprehensive study guide for all Christians—specially designed for individual or group Bible studies.

Contents

Instructions On How To Use This Workbook

1. You must be born again—have a personal relationship with the Lord Jesus Christ first, without which you cannot answer the call of God effectively to please the Master Jesus. Without Jesus, it is impossible to run this Christian race—you cannot work for somebody you do not know. For you to work for anyone there has to be a connection somehow. This is the key for effective calling and ministry—receive Jesus as your Lord and personal Savior first.

2. Your conviction plays a vital role in answering the call of God. You need to be convinced that you want to work for God. Prayerfully commit all your plans and ministrations into the hands of God and let him be in charge of all your movements and thoughts. Allowing the Holy Spirit to play his part in your life is very important as well—surrender to the leadership of the Holy Spirit.

3. Set aside a special time each day for your studies—you need to make out time and a suitable environment to avoid distractions. Get your study tools ready; your Bible, journal, pen—a concordance would be helpful too for more references. Study this workbook when your mind is alert and you have rested your body very well. You need to be in a sound condition both spiritually and physically—free from any distractions to allow you time alone with God.

4. Pray and ask the Holy Spirit to come and feed you, as you are ready to eat from his table. Pray as the Spirit of God leads and gives you utterance.

5. Do not try to go through the whole chapters at once, as that would be overwhelming. Be careful not to focus your attention on how many chapters you were able to finish at any study time rather, focus on the impact the study would make in your life both physically and spiritually. Go at your pace and by the leading of the Holy Spirit.

6. Try not to skip any chapter—it would be helpful when you go in order of the chapters. Make sure you have a clear knowledge of the previous chapters and lessons before moving forward.

7. After you have completed this workbook, it would be of great benefit to go back to it from time to time for references. This is a call for your life which is not a temporary call but rather a lifetime call, and as long as you live for Jesus.

8. Put to practice all you have learned and always depend on the Holy Spirit to lead and guide you in all your ways. May God Almighty show you favor in your walk with him in Jesus' name. Amen. God bless.

CHAPTER ONE

What is The Call of God?

In the Old Testament, there were many dedications involved as a sign of commitment on the part of both the people and the priests as well. For them to seek the face of the LORD, they had to dedicate themselves. For every child of God, there has to be that sense of commitment in your life to do the work of God.

Dedication to the service of God is required for effective call of God in your life. If you want to serve God out of a sincere heart, you need to surrender, commit your whole life to God and his work.

Your ability to submit to him in obedience brings blessings in your life. As you continue to obey and yield to the Holy Spirit, God will use you diversely in his kingdom to deliver and to save lives—God is God, and he chooses to do anything for his own glory. I encourage you to be open before the Spirit of God to direct your steps and what he will do through you will be immeasurable. Obedience to God and his word comes through humility—obedience and humility work in harmony to bring about the purpose of God for you. Bringing yourself under the control and leadership of the Holy Spirit is the beginning of your victory over the enemy and your ability to abide and follow through will bring to manifestation his blessings upon you.

OBEDIENCE

From these verses discuss obedience and how it applies to us.
John 14:15

Romans 6:16

Psalm 119:10

SUBMISSION
What is submission and how can we submit to God?
James 4:7

DEDICATION
What is dedication and in what ways can we dedicate our lives to God?
Numbers 7:89

2 Chronicles 7:9–12

Ezra 6:16

Nehemiah 12:27

WHO ARE CALLED?

Those who have received Jesus as their Lord and personal Savior—this is the basic call. After this basic call, you advance into higher calling daily as you continue to dedicate and yield yourself to the Holy Spirit to use you. Your availability to the Holy Spirit gives him more room to commission and use you always until your mission is completed.

God's calling is for those who have already known him. He will not call a stranger to work for him in his vineyard except he chooses to do so knowing that he is God and he can do whatever that pleases him. However, in a normal circumstance, he will not call a stranger to work for him. He will call those that have tasted him and have seen that he is the Lord of lords. If you love God and obey his word you are called and his love shines upon you daily.

From these verses, do you count yourself as one called by God?

John 1:12

John 3:3

John 3:16

Romans 8:14

HOW DO YOU KNOW YOU ARE CALLED?

As soon as you have received the Lord as your Savior, the Holy Spirit begins to guide you into all truth and righteousness. Only the Spirit of God bears witness to you that you are his and you will know it because he is truth. Because you love the Lord, there will be that zeal, enthusiasm to live for him always and to do his will. The Bible says in John 6:37, "All that the Father giveth me shall come to me; and him that cometh to me I will in no wise cast out."

From these verses, how can you know God has called you?

John 14:26

John 16:8–13

Luke 12:12

Romans 8:15–16, 26

Isaiah 30:21

Discussion question: Tell your story how you finally decided you were called into the ministry.

CHAPTER TWO

Reasons Why Some Believers Struggle With The Call of God

MIND-SET

From these scripture verses, what does the scripture say concerning the state of your mind? How can your mind be put right?

Romans 12:1–2

Philippians 2:5

Philippians 4:8

Colossians 3:2

James 4:3

Isaiah 26:3

WAITING FOR SUCH A TIME

What are the dangers you might encounter when you wait for such a time in answering the call of God?

Discuss these scripture verses.
Ecclesiastes 11:4

Romans 11:29

EXCUSES

Sometimes people give excuses for what they did and why. However, God does not accept any excuses rather he wants you to do his work though he will never force you to do it anyway. If you sinned because someone pushed you to the wall, you are still responsible for your actions. It does not matter what made you sin. God wants every individual to live above sin no matter what. Resist the devil in any manner he tends to manifest in your way—your ability to resist is your victory. Satan will try to fight you but do not yield to his temptations. We are born to win not by our own strength but by the power of Christ Jesus—very important to note. God will not honor you for blaming anyone, ministers, parents, friends, congregation, or even situations and circumstances for sinning. Therefore, sit up and contend for your salvation because it is very expensive and you cannot afford to lose it for any reason.

Mention the people who gave excuses from these scripture passages.
Matthew 19:21–22

Luke 9:59

Luke 9:61

Genesis 3:12–13

Exodus 32:22–23

1 Samuel 15:13–15, 20–21

What are your excuses for not answering the call of God today? Name them.

After you have named them, ask God to forgive you and have mercy on you because none of your excuses is legitimate enough before God though they are for you. It does not make any sense to God when you present your personal issues as an excuse for not doing his work. He is the commander in chief of your life if you let him. You can still choose not to do what he says, and it will be your choice too. However, I encourage you to obey God, and it shall be well with you in Jesus' name. Amen.

INABILITY TO BRING THE SPIRITUAL INTO THE PHYSICAL

Things of the spirit take only the spiritual being to understand them. When there is no understanding of that which God has revealed, there is trouble, confusion and lack of peace or you can even ignore it. The Bible says in John 4:24, "God is a Spirit: and they that worship him must worship him in spirit and in truth."

From these verses, what happens when one is not able to interpret the spiritual?

Daniel 2:1–6

Daniel 5:5–10

ANSWERED THE WRONG CALL

The choices you make and the directions you take could be far from the route God wants you to take. Sometimes some people know the direction God wants them to take but refuse it because it does not fit to their desires. When God commands you to do something and you refuse to do it the way he wants but instead you did it your own way, it is considered pure disobedient. Answering the wrong call could be because of your disobedient or lack of dedication to God on your own part. Walking and doing things your own way could be dangerous and might cause you to suffer afflictions in the hands of the enemy and losing your blessings from God as well. Be watchful and let the Lord lead you in all so that it may be well with you. Adam and Eve were to eat every other fruit except one, and this was their call at that time in conjunction with taking care of the garden. However, the enemy came through the wife and the call and plan of God did not happen the way God had purposed it. The enemy does not want the call of God for your life to happen hence, he strives to put a barrier between you and God through sin.

However, it will be your own responsibility to say no to Satan as you stand firm to fight this battle by obeying the command of God. You cannot be passive rather you need to be a solider so that the purpose and plan of God for your life will come to pass. Samson did the same as he gave in to the enemy to stand against the plan and purpose of God for his life. He was supposed to be a Nazarene and someone to deliver his people Israel. However, compromise crept in as he began to experience defeat from the enemy followed by his fall. He started breaking the rule of his calling as a Nazarene when he ate the honey from the dead lion and gave his parents some without telling them how he got it. Furthermore, the devil manifested his deception spirit through Delilah to him because of his fleshly lust. You cannot bargain with the devil or even give any room to converse with him. Satan is the father of all liars and he will make sure you are subdued because you gave him room first to come in. The only thing you need to do is to command Satan to get behind you and he will flee. Jesus overcame Satan therefore, you can overcome him too by God's power.

In addition, Lot's wife stumbled as well—she was not supposed to look back but she did. She might have been thinking about all their possessions they have left behind. She seems to have valued those possessions more than the word of God hence her defeat. All these distractions come from no other source but from the devil. He is very tactful in finding means of attacking God's children. Do not take any chances or take the devil for granted saying he has no power—devil has power but God's power is greater than his. God did not take away his power from Satan when he disobeyed him and thrown down from heaven. However, God's power is greater than his. So do not eat with him or go closer because he is deceitful and wants to get many people as possible into hell with him. His mission is to make sure the purpose of God for your life did not come to pass.

What are possible consequences for answering the wrong call?

Discuss these scripture passages.

Genesis 2:16–17

Genesis 3:1–6

Genesis 19:17, 26

Judges 13:3–5

Judges 14: 1-3, 6–9

Judges 16:6–9

Judges 16:10–12

Judges 16:13–14

Judges 16:15–18

Judges 16:19–20

IMITATION

Seek the face of God in everything and he will show you what to do. Walking directly in God's leadership will save you from so many problems than just copying other people. Sometimes, what you see in the physical might not be exactly what it is in the spiritual. Those people you might be imitating could be walking in deceit and not being real. They might not be operating under the direct leadership of the Holy Spirit. They could misconstrue or even misinterpret the message or vision God gave them or worse yet starting outright but misses along the way. Do not be deceived with the physical rather seek God and he will channel your ways.

How can a believer seek the Lord in the light of these scriptures?

Deuteronomy 4:29

Jeremiah 29:13

Jeremiah 33:3

Hosea 10:12

Galatians 5:25

POSITIONING AND TIMING

How could positioning and timing affect your walk with God? (Positive or negative)

Do you agree that God is a master planner?   **YES __NO __**
What are these scripture passages saying?
1 Samuel 9:5–6

1 Samuel 9:15–16

1 Samuel 9:19–20

1 Samuel 9:22–23

1 Samuel 9:25–27

1 Samuel 10:1

Ruth 1:12, 16–18

Ruth 2:1–11

Ecclesiastes 9:11

Have you seen God manifest in your life as a master planner? Share.

LACK OF FAITH IN GOD

What does the scripture say concerning lack of faith from these verses?
Matthew 13:58

Matthew 14:31

Matthew 17:20

Matthew 21:21

ANGER

Discuss these scriptures about anger.

Psalm 37:8

Proverbs 14:17, 29

Proverbs 16:32

Ecclesiastes 7:9

Matthew 5:22

Ephesians 4:26-27, 31–32

James 1:19–20

FEAR OF THE UNKNOWN

What can cause anyone to be afraid from these scriptures?

Joshua 1:9

Psalm 27:1–2

Psalm 56:3–4

Proverbs 3:5

Isaiah 41:10, 13

Isaiah 54:4

Matthew 10:26

2 Timothy 1:7

NEGLECTING THE CHANNEL AND OPPORTUNITY GOD HAS PROVIDED
Discuss these scripture passages.
Matthew 25:42–45

John 9:4

John 12:35

Galatians 6:10

Ephesians 5:16

How can we overcome the spirit of negligence in the Christendom today?

LACK OF UNDERSTANDING OF GOD'S VISIONS AND REVELATIONS
Discuss these scripture verses.
Job 33:14

Proverbs 29:18

Hosea 4:6

Ephesians 1:17–18

FAULTY FOUNDATION

Why is foundation very important in the life of a believer?

What is the scripture saying about foundation from these verses?
Psalm 82:5

Proverbs 10:25

Matthew 7:26:27

1 Corinthians 3:11

CHAPTER THREE

Some Characters in The Bible Who Struggled
in Answering The Call of God

MOSES

What are his struggles from these verses?
Exodus 3:11–12

Exodus 3:13–16

Exodus 4:1–9

Exodus 4:13–17

BARAK

What are his Struggles from these verses?
Judges 4:6–9

GIDEON

What are his struggles from these verses?
Judges 6:12–13

Judges 6:14–15

Judges 6:16:26

JEREMIAH

What are his struggles from these verses?
Jeremiah 1:4–10

JONAH

What are his struggles from these verses?
Jonah 1:1–3

BALAAM

What are his struggles from these verses?
Numbers 22:9–14

WHAT IS PERFECT WILL OF GOD? (GOD'S OWN WILL)

Perfect will of God as the name sounds means perfect as you will not find any error or grounds for regrets at the end. It also means when you allow God to decide for you and not you deciding for yourself. You do all the things God wants you to do without adding any of your own thoughts or ideas. In the case of Balaam, God specifically told him not to go with the messengers sent by Balak. This was the will of God for him.

WHAT IS PERMISSIVE WILL OF GOD? (YOUR OWN PERSONAL WILL)

(See Numbers 22:9,20). Permissive will of God means when God allows you to do things the way that fits your own taste and desire. In this case, it is your own decision, the choice to do as you wished, and you have not sinned against God by so doing. Permissive on the other hand, means that you could do something as you wished but that does not mean it is your best choice. Balaam wanted to go and God later allowed him to go since that was what he chose to do to satisfy himself rather than God. It is very important that you take cognizance your motives of doing whatever you are doing or want to do for God. Your motive determines the outcome of whatever you do in life. (I Sam 8:4–7), The Jews demanded for a king just to be like other nations.

PETER

What are his struggles from these verses?
Acts 10:9–20

John 21:15–24

What are your own struggles for not answering the call of God for your life?

Pray about them and ask God for his grace to surrender totally.

Are there lessons to learn from these prophets above?

CHAPTER FOUR

Faulty Foundation

Faulty foundation that already exists in one's life does not manifest without something triggering it. It comes up when you sin against God or your salvation. At some other times when someone wants to start a ministry, it seems as if the devil and his agents have been let loose to fight you—if you persevere victory is yours. Several factors could trigger faulty foundation in the life of any person. Every individual is different and dealings of God are different as well. It could be just a very little thing, as little as a comment you made to somebody could trigger the already existing faulty foundation to begin to manifest. I recall when my dad called for one of his solemn family meetings to tell them about my decisions to marry my husband. After he had ruled his verdict, I said, well, I know this is from God and I "must" obey the will of God. This was as if a very strong bomb was released in our midst—it was horrible. When I said it, I did not have any intention to hurt or humiliate anybody. I was very polite as I explained my convictions. My dad rose from his chair and began to display. Though things have been happening but he never knew that I would stand before him to say, I must obey God. Well, I said it. The human eyes can only see thus far in the physical. My dad knew exactly why he flared up. God out of his divine power and ordination knew that my marriage was going to be an issue after I had declared I must. As a child of God, you should be able to stand on your conviction from God no matter what—he alone is the highest authority. My dad thought because he is my father, he has every right to do whatever he wanted with me. He can because he has power and authority over us as a parent. However, because I believe in Jesus Christ through whom I have been justified by faith, he has no such power to proclaim any evil upon me anymore—Jesus. However, any of his children who do not believe in Christ, he has that right as a father to hold such captive. This is faulty foundation in full force that was hidden but suddenly sprang up alive. There has to be a channel for the already existing faulty foundation to be in full operation.

SOME CHANNELS THROUGH WHICH FAULTY FOUNDATION OPERATES

FAMILY INFLUENCE

First, a family that has any of her members previously or currently worshipping idol or strange gods other than God Almighty is under a curse. Except every one of them receives Christ, otherwise it will be a very big battle for any believer who springs up.

In addition, for every scripture you disobey you are under a curse as well. The Bible says in Galatians 3:10, "For as many as are of the works of the law are under the curse: for it is written, cursed is every one that continueth not in all things which are written in the book of the law to do them." Family foundation is very important in the life of someone whether Christian or non-Christian. Family has a very huge influence in the life of anybody. When you are born into a family, you are bound to learn beginning from your infancy stage. You are under the authority of your parents; it does not matter whether biological or adopted parents. Your caregivers matter as well both spiritually and physically. Your personality plays an important role too in your upbringing and people around as well. As you grow, you begin to explore your surroundings and whatever you have been introduced to is what you would follow. However, it will be your choice to do certain things you have learned from the family or not. By the time you can deduce from what is right or wrong, you can now decide for yourself which route you would go. If you grew up in a non-Christian home and learned about God somehow, it will be your decision to follow him or not. However, the essential point I am trying to make here is that your family somehow influences the level and degree of your struggle, and success coupled with the exposure and the environment under which you were raised. Consider a Christian home and a non-Christian home. In a Christian home, parents pray over their children daily and profess blessings over their lives, future homes, families, career, ministry and prosperity in everything. When these children grow up, they have fewer struggles in life in everything because somebody dedicated their time to pray for them continually. In addition, those children who remain faithful to the Lord and walk in obedience to God receive the grace of God in their lives. You will see some ministers prospering in their ministries not because they are more prayerful but because someone prayed for them before, and God honored their prayers—godly parents or guardian. That is what God can do—he answers every prayer of his children. I have even seen people fallen away from the faith but because their parents are faithfully following God, his mercy sustained them even when they did not deserve it. He protected and kept them because of their parents—God is a God of covenant. He keeps his covenant onto generation to generation especially to them who are faithful to him. On the other hand, children who were brought up under cursing every single day and night—the parents never for once proclaimed blessings of any kind upon them all their lives instead they received curses. Such children grow up in life struggling for everything until God intervenes. Sometimes they may end up committing suicide or become useless if they cannot handle the stress anymore especially those that have not embraced Christ in their lives. However, they that know their God and continually put their trust in him shall be delivered. However, they have to fight it out through prayers otherwise; it would not be fun and easy. I am a living testimony of someone growing up without being blessed for one day by my father irrespective of all I did to serve and honor him as a father. Instead of blessings, I received curses. If there were any means of measuring the amount and weight of curses that my own biological father had laid upon me, you would be astounded. Even when I thought we had reconciled, and he came to our home, he continued from where he had stopped—cursing and heaps of them indeed. This is pure representation and manifestation of Satan in his traditional attire. This shows you the extent Satan can go to destroy your life when you strongly believe in God. Those demons will manifest with full force to wage war against you. Do not give up brethren for our God is mighty. I have and serve a mighty God of Power, a God of Righteousness and a God of Justice—he has never let me down. If not God my story would have ended on this earth but praise God for Jesus—I love my dad but Satan I hate. By the blood of Jesus Christ of Nazareth who died and suffered for us on the cross, I am free from those curses from the beginning to the end. I am a blessed woman called and chosen by God. I have struggled without question; however, God allowed it for the sake of the precious lives in the family so they might come to the true light. God sometimes does not just waive things like that because if he does, you might not even have a clue of what he did—he wants you to know that he can do all things.

Consequently, for the battle between the devil and us, have you wondered why God allowed Satan to continue to attack his children instead of him wiping Satan away immediately? Have you ever thought of that? God can blink his eyes, and Satan will just die and be no more. I asked God the same question too. However, he does not want to do that. He gave me the impression that we need to contend for our faith—Christian race is called a battle, and we all know Satan to be our enemy and why he is fighting us—Righteousness from God—Satan hates this. I never forget this hence it is in my everyday language—you have to fight to win. If it were easy, Jesus would not have died. God would have just given a command, and that would do it. So do not give up for God is in control of us. Amen.

Discuss these scriptures below.

Exodus 20:3–5

Proverbs 22:6

SALVATION

Why is salvation very important?

John 3:3

1 Peter 3:15

Deuteronomy 10:12–13

1 Samuel 12:24

1 John 5:18

INABILITY TO HEAR AND UNDERSTAND THE VOICE OF GOD

If a believer does not hear the voice of God, it is a very big faulty foundation. Imagine you have a child and that child fails to recognize your voice as the parent when you call. Would you consider that as normal? Not at all rather, you would conclude that something is wrong. If you call yourself a true child of God and cannot hear the voice of God, something is wrong. You need to pray and break anything standing against you from penetrating into the spirit to hear the voice of God. The devil stands in the way to put a stumbling block because when you hear and understand the voice of God and are willing to obey him, your life will be transformed, and God's name will be glorified. You need to be able to have a smooth communication with your heavenly Father so it might be well with you.

DISOBEDIENCE

What is the command of God to Adam from this verse?
Genesis 2:17

How did Adam respond to God?
Genesis 3:6

What is the command of the LORD to Saul from this verse?
1 Samuel 15:3

How did Saul respond to the LORD?
1 Samuel 15:9

What is the command of the LORD to Jonah from this verse?
Jonah 1:2

How did Jonah respond to the LORD?
Jonah 1:3

CONSEQUENCES OF DISOBEDIENCE
What are the consequences of disobedience from these scripture passages?
Genesis 3:14–15

Genesis 3:16

Genesis 3:17–19

Genesis 3:23–24

1 Samuel 15:10

1 Samuel 15:23b

1 Samuel 15:28

1 Samuel 15:35c

SPIRIT OF ACCUSATIONS

Satan is the one who accuses the children of God before God. He questions God for protecting us his children, and because he protects us; he thinks that is why we chose to serve him. God permitted Satan to go and trouble Job but commanded him not to touch his life. Satan struck Job to make sure he curses God but he remained faithful to God. The same Satan that attacked Job and all his possessions is alive and well in our days today—he is still doing the same thing to us. However, do not give up God will grant you victory in the end. All along, Job had no idea what was going on behind the scene that Satan was accusing him before God and that God was proud of him. Satan is always seeking for channels, occasions and avenues to accuse children of God. This is his primary job so he can come in to attack—Brethren, Satan is all over you. Though you do not see him, he has agents working for him non-stop. Making yourself available to the enemy to use you to accuse or pass judgment on your fellow is not godly. The Bible says in 2 Timothy 2:19, "Nevertheless the foundation of God standeth sure, having this seal, The Lord knoweth them that are his. And, Let every one that nameth the name of Christ depart from iniquity."

What can you say from these verses?

Job 1:6–7

Job 1:9–11

Job 2:1–2

Job 2:4–6

Revelation 12:10

Zechariah 3:1

ALWAYS BEING ACCUSED

When you are always being accused and people finding fault with you for no reason, it is a faulty foundation. Christ Jesus paid the price on the cross for any kind of oppression of the enemy anyone might have. Christ has justified you because you believe in him. The devil uses this avenue to fight against you in the physical. This is different from the battle that goes on daily between God and Satan on your behalf. When the spiritual accusation is completed, then it manifests on the physical and that is why the Christian race is a huge battle twenty-four hours until Jesus comes. The Bible already told us to watch and pray always. Prayer should not be seasonal but continuously all the days of our lives. Now that you are facing this mark of accusation, you have to fight it out through prayers. In the spiritual world you have a mark of the enemy. This mark is how they recognize or denote you as they have their agents planted strategically everywhere you go to fulfill their evil mission in your life. You have to plead the blood of Jesus upon your life and delete whatever mark of recognition from the spiritual world. That is why sometimes you see people getting into trouble of all sorts. When the trouble comes though you are innocent but I tell you, it will take the grace of God for you to come out of it. If you are taken unawares even those you think are your friend will speak against you. When this curse is against you, the route you took and had problems, if someone else takes that same route they are fine and no trouble will ever surface. Detach yourself from such it is of the devil—through prayers and having the knowledge of what is going on, God will deliver you. Before I got married, my dad used to have serious accidents at certain seasons. This was not normal but rather the oppression of the enemy. However, by the special grace of God through prayers it was resolved. Sometimes if you do not know your right as a child of God, the enemy takes advantage of you.

Furthermore, some believers use curse interchangeably with judgment or make some argument with or between the two. However, it is clear that whatever judgment passed or curses laid on someone are as a result of disobedience, which sometimes passes from hand to hand or from generation to generation. When it is from the Lord or his word, it is just and righteous altogether but outside of this comes from the evil one.

Discuss these scriptures?

Acts 13:39

Romans 8:33

Galatians 2:16

CHAPTER FIVE

Curses, Kinds and How They Operate

What is a curse?

Who can lay a curse?

What are the conditions for curses to be effective in the life of anyone?

Can curses be effective in the life of a true child of God?   Yes__ No__
Why and why not?

PROVERBS 26:2 (VERY IMPORTANT SCRIPTURE TO NOTE).

What did you understand from this verse?

Romans 8:33
What does this passage really mean to you?

2 Corinthians 5:17
Is this particular scripture verse true in your life?

Do you have to believe or fear any kind of curses from anywhere?

What are you supposed to do if you feel cursed or realized someone has laid a curse (s) on you?

Share your experience or testimony of deliverance from any kind of curses.

However, this is the word of God, which cannot be broken. All the curses that seem to be manifesting in your life have its base from these Bible verses. Disobedient to the word of God brings them to full manifestation. Deuteronomy 28 has the whole range of life expounded. Deuteronomy 28:16–68, Exodus 20:2–6 and Exodus 34:6–7.

Discuss these scriptures.

Deuteronomy 28:16–68

Exodus 20:2–6

Exodus 34:6–7

When you are operating under the old covenant of the law, these curses definitely have greater effect and influence in your life. However, when you come into the new covenant through the blood of Jesus Christ, it cannot have any effect in your life anymore. However, might surface but victory comes through Christ Jesus to prove his supremacy over all other powers? For instance, since I was born into a family that had some of its members worship strange gods, is a curse for the whole family. God chose his own even before they were conceived. I am very sure that God laughed at them to scorn the day he formed me because he already knew there would be war and battle to fight. In addition, he knew as well that he would win the battle. If you read my story carefully, faulty foundation was originally triggered immediately I gave my life to Jesus Christ—now power has changed hands. All those idols and strange gods have seen the greater power in authority hence my battle and afflictions. However, the blood of Jesus is greater and more powerful than them. These demons are rebels like their father **Satan.**

Therefore, God has done us well by sending his Son to die for us so those curses can have no effect on us any longer—sin can open the door again anyway. When you are not faithful to God and swimming in sin—you will surely be in trouble. God is a God of righteousness. For full victory in this warfare with Satan and his agents, you need to be fully dedicated to God if you have some kind of family curses. Some people ignore it and take it for granted but their end has proved them wrong a time and again.

However, for these curses, the blood of Jesus has paid for them all on the cross if you believe. They will never have any effect in your life anymore. However, it would be your choice to follow the truth if your family foundation was not built on the truth, which is Christ Jesus. It does matter what has happened or what is happening now in your family. The moment you recognize that things are not right, begin to ask God for direction; he will lead, and direct you to make sure the enemy standing on your spiritual and physical life is demolished. As you read on these curses, if you feel you have been cursed and oppressed; pray and claim your victory in Jesus' name. Amen. On the cross of Calvary, Jesus bore all our iniquities; sicknesses and diseases, poverty, untimely deaths, accusations of all sorts, Christ has paid for them all—claim victory in place of curses. Jabez cried onto God because his name was walking against him. He prayed to God with all his heart and God manifested. God does not change he is still the same yesterday, today and forever therefore, pray, and cry out to God Almighty—he will answer you. "And Jabez called on the God of Israel, saying, Oh that thou wouldest bless me indeed, and enlarge my coast, and that thine hand might be with me, and that thou wouldest keep me from evil, that it may not grieve me! And God granted him that which he requested" (1 Chronicles 4:10).

GENERATIONAL CURSE OF HATERS OF THE GOSPEL OF JESUS CHRIST

Do you find yourself not being able to love God and his word even when you try to do it you find yourself falling back? Do you find yourself not having any interest in the things of God and Christianity? On the other hand, are you just being neutral or even thinking about believing in something else other than God Almighty? Pray, it is not by your own making—forces of darkness behind these. It is not the Spirit of God of course rather of the devil. Begin to pray and bind such powers and let God work in you to destroy those things, which the enemy has done, and you shall be free in Jesus' name. Amen.

Discuss these scriptures

Exodus 23:25

Deuteronomy 6:5

Deuteronomy 10: 12

Deuteronomy 11:1

Matthew 22:37

Mark 12:3

Luke 10:27

GENERATIONAL CURSE OF UNTIMELY DEATH

When people in your family die at a young age it is not of God. It does not matter what led to the death. Satan is always ready to give a name to anything just to make you believe his lies. I recall when my mother started having her trouble from which she finally passed away—Satan gave it a name. However, during those times I was not a believer—was still in bondage of the enemy. I did not even have any insight overall with the spiritual matters hence she was afflicted. Had it been today my mother would not have died yet, not sure, what the will of God would have been. However, even at that God would have delivered her without any human effort but he chose not to for reasons best known to him. You see God is God, he chooses to do whatever that pleases him. I know I had asked God so many questions about the death of my mother that he refused to answer me which made me to be angry with him and finally ended me into trouble in his hands. When you are dealing with someone greater than you are in everything, you have no choice than to surrender otherwise you end up being in more troubles. However, after many troubles, I have learned to surrender all to God because he is all knowing and we cannot question or challenge his authority. God does so many things that might not make sense to us sometimes as humans but he knows the best. I would have loved my precious mother to enjoy us her children and see her grandchildren, which she so much desired.

Consequently, the enemy fought her and God allowed the enemy to prevail against her—if he did not allow her death, it would not have happened but he allowed it anyway. This is one of the unfortunate situations that one has to let God be God—so unfortunate. Well, that is just what it is—when you do not know, you allow God to take charge because he knows it all and every secret is open before him.

Therefore, anything contrary to the word of God in your life is a curse. God has promised all his children long life. If you die or your family members die young, all being equal—is not a good sign. Furthermore, not only will you live longer but in good health and enjoy the works of his creation hence it does not make sense to live longer under sicknesses and torment of health issues. Therefore, you "must" be in good health free from afflictions and oppressions of Satan in your body. For you to have a long life, you must abide under the shadow of the LORD Almighty in obedience and in his righteousness. The devil will never fulfill his wicked desires in your life in Jesus' name. Amen.

Discuss these scripture verses.

Genesis 15:15

Exodus 20:12

1 Kings 3:14

Job 5:26

Psalm 91:16

Psalm 118:17

Psalm 128:6

Proverbs 10:27

Ephesians 6:2–3

Proverbs 16:31

GENERATIONAL CURSE OF SICKNESSES AND DISEASES

When you are being afflicted with one sickness or the other, it is not from God especially when a particular sickness goes from one hand to the other—a curse needed to be broken. The Bible says in the book of James 5:14–16, "Is any sick among you? let him call for the elders of the church; and let them pray over him, anointing him with oil in the name of the Lord: And the prayer of faith shall save the sick, and the Lord shall raise him up; and if he have committed sins, they shall be forgiven him. Confess your faults one to another, that ye may be healed. The effectual fervent prayer of a righteous man availeth much." Covering your sins will not do you any good but when you confess them and you shall be healed in Jesus' name. Amen.

Discuss these scripture verses.

Exodus 15:26

Exodus 23:25

Exodus 34:10

48

Isaiah 53:5

GENERATIONAL CURSE OF HATRED

The story between Cain and Abel is a good example in the Bible that shows the effect of a generational curse in the life of anyone if not broken (See Genesis chapter 4). Adam and Eve disobeyed God and were thrown out of the Garden of Eden—their first two children were Cain and Abel. Adam and Eve committed the sin of disobedience, which transferred from their hands to their children and to all humanity today on this earth—sin. Cain out of jealousy and hatred killed his brother. This puts him under more curses including the ones he inherited from his parents—one sin leads to another. God said in Exodus 20:13, "Thou shalt not kill." He did it and disobeyed God. Remember for any word of God you disobey you are under a curse. There was no reason why Cain should kill his brother instead of loving him. That is a faulty foundation. The family did not start well in the LORD because of sin, and it is continuing as Cain was cursed and he was miserable. Even in his state, he still did not realize that what he did was not normal—concerned with his punishment. Abel was hated for no just reason. Everybody has a right to serve God the way they want. Abel chose the way that he felt was best for him and Cain did the same for himself. Abel died just because of the faulty foundation in their family. Look at my own self. My dad hated me just because I want to get married. Remember that my dad's family had a terrible faulty foundation because of the worship of idol—strange gods. Terrible! Terrible! Terrible! Now by the grace of God I was saved to mention the name of Jesus in that family, and it was as if—who is this stranger. We had better do something about it before they overthrow us those demons thought. I am telling you today that their kingdom has been divided, and I am proud of Jesus that in my generation, those curses have been broken by the power of God. If not the blood of Jesus, I would have been the most miserable talk less of having the breath of life—kill me as they did to my mother, or I remain alive but were better dead. Brethren I thank Jesus so much that he loves me even in my unfaithfulness he saved me, delivered me and gave me hope and a future. Thank you my LORD for your unconditional love for your children. I am no better than my mother was but he chose to keep me. I have chosen to follow him Master Jesus until I am no more.

Discuss these scripture verses?

Genesis 4:3–8

Genesis 12:3

Psalm 37:23–24

Proverbs 16:7

GENERATIONAL CURSE OF POVERTY

It is not the will of God that any of his children should lack any good thing or lack daily bread. You work hard but receive less—no matter what you try to do they collapse on the way. You find out that you are not the only individual in your family suffering from the same problems. As people grow up in the family, they continue to face the same difficulties even in a greater dimension. For instance, in a family of four, only one person could keep a job and able to keep the rest of the family going and even at that it is a struggle in all areas. Oh! No, no, something is wrong somewhere.

Furthermore, when you cannot keep a job for any reason that is not from God. You secure a job today, for some reasons you are laid off or something happened the job could not exist anymore. Pray God to deliver your life because you are in bondage of the enemy—does not matter how you lose it or what caused it. Remember what I said earlier that Satan always finds a name to give to situations to make you believe his lies. The inability of any household to meet up with their daily needs, and this progresses from one hand to the other even from generation to generation is a curse. Pray and plead the blood of Jesus and he will deliver you—the word of God is for you to believe, claim and make use of it.

However, when you stuck yourself up with the lies of the enemy, as hopeless as Satan is, he will continue to keep you miserable. I hate Satan, and he hates me too—he tortured me when I was still in darkness. Do not let him for he is a miserable foe. He will end in the bottomless pit one of these days. God will always help his children for sure. Keep on going forward, we must overcome by the blood of Jesus. One of the ways to overcome this curse of poverty is, always pay your tithe. When you are cursed with poverty, the enemy finds a channel to come in to trigger the existing faulty foundation in your life. If you rob God, there is no way for God to rebuke the devourer for your sake. I encourage you to pay your tithe, and God will fight for you. My dad said to me. "You think you have money? That money you have will be gone from your hands." You see I have gone through so much with my dad, and every of his words I take them serious because I know he meant every one of them. One of my brothers said when things went out of hand again, "Chinyere the case between you and dede I cannot put my mouth anymore you both settle—you are tough and dede is tough." I laughed. (Dede is what we call our dad). My dad and I are representing two opposite kingdoms that are strong in power. However, in the end the strongest will defeat the opponent. I thought our case was over, apparently not from the trend of things as we are continuing in the battle until the weakest surrenders. Indeed, before the foundation of the earth, it is settled in heaven, even our victory that is why I continue to wait for the full manifestation of God's own time. Amen. I am confident without question or doubt that God Almighty is the commander in authority. He will never give up on his own as long as they continue to persevere. All these curses mentioned in this book have been laid upon me in the highest degree and more that are not even mentioned or written down. However, the blood of Jesus has set me free though at a certain point in my life they seem to be manifesting or being active. Sometimes God allows you to experience certain things so you can learn your lessons in the end. God proved that he is God the creator of heaven and earth. God is my strong tower, the only weapon I have and for all believers; he is our weapon—in him we are safe. Our God is mighty and greater than any other power. Hallelujah! Fear him and serve him, he will surely deliver you. I have seen his faithfulness in my life, in the life of my husband and our children. He is the only reason we are still living today. Please thank God for us for power has gone out of God to deliver us greatly. If not for the mercies of God you will not be reading this book today. Therefore, I have every reason to serve Him—I am alive.

Discuss these scripture passages.

Genesis 22:12–14, 17, 18

Psalm 23:1

Psalm 34:10

Psalm 37:25

Psalm 84:11

GENERATIONAL CURSE IN MARRIAGE

The only way to be free from this curse and many others is through the blood of Jesus. There is no magic about it. Christ Jesus has paid the price on the cross for all humanity. Whether you have been cursed that you will never get married or even when you get married that you shall be barren, these will never exist for you if you do not believe the lies of the enemy. However, you have to call upon the name of the Lord and you shall be saved. When you marry you have not sinned but if you choose not to marry you have not sinned either. Nevertheless, if you want to marry and cannot have the right person; facing disappointments or married people facing divorce, barrenness, definitely, these are contrary to the will of God for your life.

Discuss these scripture verses.

Genesis 1:27

Genesis 2:24

Genesis 9:7

Exodus 23:26

Proverbs 10:22

Mark 10:7

1 Corinthians 7:9

1 Corinthians 7:36–38

Ephesians 5:31

GENERATIONAL CURSE OF BARRENNESS

Barrenness is not for any child of God. Any situation that is contrary to the word of God is a curse, and it will be your sole responsibility to understand that such are not from God and seek the face of God. The word of God must be fulfilled in the lives of God's children and anything that wants to oppose it must bow in the name of Jesus. Prayers can change situations—when you pray and believe God, he comes down to deliver. God answered prayers of many in the Bible days and that same God is alive forevermore; he will do the same for us if we believe and call upon him with a sincere heart.

Deuteronomy 15:14
What are the promises of God to his children from this Bible verse?

Psalm 113:9
What is the promise of God to his children from this Bible verse?

Genesis 16:1–2, 18:11
What is happening from these verses?

Genesis 18:10, 14
What is the promise of God to them?

Genesis 21:1–3
Did God fulfill his promises?

1 Samuel 1:2, 5–7
What is happening from these verses?

1Samuel 1:10–11
What did Hannah do?

1 Samuel 1:20
Did God answer her prayers?

I Samuel 2:1–2
What was Hannah's countenance after?

Luke 1:5, 7
What was happening from these verses?

Luke 1:13–16
What were the promises of God to them?

Luke 1:24, 57
Did God fulfill his promises to them?

PRAYER REQUEST

Pray for as many that are in need of the fruit of the womb both known and unknown.

Ask God to have mercy upon them.

Destroy every work of the enemy fighting against their lives and pray for the promises of God to come to pass in their lives. Thank God for victory in Jesus' name. Amen.

We have good news from God through Christ Jesus who sacrificed his life for us that through him; we might have new life. God can change situations and make the crooked road to be straight again. Claim the promises of God and it shall be well with you in Jesus' name. Amen.

What are the promises of God for his children from these verses?
Leviticus 26:39–42

Deuteronomy 7:15

Deuteronomy 24:16

Deuteronomy 30:19–20

Job 5:26

Psalm 118: 17

Psalm 128:6

Proverbs 16:7

Isaiah 53:5

Ezekiel 18:20–21

Galatians 3:13

BREAK THROUGH PRAYERS OVER FAULTY FOUNDATION

Write out all the areas you need God to intervene in your personal life, family, church and in the world today. List them out and pray about them until God grants you victory. Do not stop knocking at the door of heaven until your burden has been lifted off your shoulder. Also, pray with this Bible verse I Chronicles 4:10, "And Jabez called on the God of Israel, saying, Oh that thou wouldest bless me indeed, and enlarge my coast, and that thine hand might be with me, and that thou wouldest keep me from evil, that it may not grieve me! And God granted him that which he requested."

CHAPTER SIX

Why Did God Call You?

TO PREACH THE GOSPEL

Which gospel are we supposed to preach?

Discuss these scripture verses.
Matthew 24:14

Luke 4:18

Luke 4:43

Isaiah 61:1

GOD IS LOVE

How did God prove his love for us and how are we supposed to love?
John 3:16

I John. 4:7-8

1 John 4:16

DISCUSSIONS:

Some take the love of God for granted; dwelling in sin continuously with the conclusion—God is love, and he understands. *(God will never understand when you disobey him always.)* Do you agree? Comments:

YOU ARE SPECIAL BEFORE GOD ALMIGHTY

Discuss these Bible verses. How are you special before God?
Genesis 1:26–27

Jeremiah 1:5

Romans 8:29–30

1 Corinthians 1:26–31

Ephesians 2:10

1 Peter 2:9–10

TO DELIVER THE OPPRESSED

How does God feel when his children are suffering oppression of the enemy? Is God able to deliver?

Discuss these scripture verses.
Genesis 21:16–19

Exodus 2:23–25

Exodus 3:7–9

Exodus 14:28–31

Exodus 6:6–7

2 Kings 13:6

Psalm 18:2

Psalm 72:12–14

Daniel 3:16–25

Romans 11:26

TO PROVE HE IS A GOD THAT ANSWERS PRAYER

Discuss these scripture verses. Does God answer prayer?

1 Samuel 1:10–13

1 Samuel 2:1–2

1 Kings 18:24, 37–39

Jonah 2:1–2

TO PROSPER HIS CHILDREN

Discuss these scripture verses. How can God prosper his children?
Genesis 12:1–3

Deuteronomy 8:18

Psalm 1:1–3

Jeremiah 29:5–7, 11

Malachi 3:10

John 10:10

Galatians 3:13–14

3 John 2

TO PROVE HE IS A GOD OF MIRACLE

What are the miracles in these scripture verses?
Matthew 9:1–8

Matthew 9:20–22

Matthew 9:18–19, 23–25

Matthew 9:27–31

Matthew 9:32–33

Matthew 9:35

Matthew 14:14–21

Matthew 14:22–33

John 2:1–9

TO PROVE HE IS A GOD OF COVENANT

Who did God make covenant with from these verses? Did God fulfill the covenant he made?

Genesis 12:1–3

Genesis 15:18

Genesis 17:1–8

Genesis 17:15–21

Genesis 26:2–4

Genesis 28:13–15

Genesis 35:10–12

TO EXPOSE THE WORKS OF THE ENEMY
Which enemy are we talking about in these verses?
John 8:44

Colossians 1:16–17

Colossians 2:15

CHAPTER SEVEN

Reasons Why God's Plan Are Sometimes Delayed

SOMEONE MIGHT BE LIVING IN SIN

Discuss these Bible verses.
1 John 3:8

Psalm 66:18

Proverbs 14:34

Proverbs 28:13

Romans 6:23

Romans 12:1–2

2 Timothy 2:19

1 John 3:8
Is it possible for one to be a Christian and yet be living in sin?

PRAYING YOUR OWN WAY INSTEAD OF GOD'S WAY
How can one pray in his or her own way? Discuss these verses.
2 Samuel 2:9

2 Chronicles 32:7–8

Psalm 20:7

Psalm 146:3–6

Matthew 6:9–13

Philippians 4:6–8

LACK OF AVAILABLE VESSEL TO BE USED

How can anyone struggle with God's will? Discuss these verses.
Exodus 3:9–11, 13

Exodus 4:1, 10, 12–13

Jonah 1:1–3

HIDDEN VISION (SIMILAR REFERENCES; MARK 8:27–31 LUKE 9:18–21)
How can a vision be hidden?

Discuss these scripture verses.
Mathew 16:13–23

Matthew 20:20–23

Proverbs 29:18

IGNORANT OF GOD'S WILL AND PLAN
Can one be ignorant of the will and plan of God for his or her life? How?

Discuss these scripture verses.
Proverbs 29:18

Hosea 4:6

Luke 12:48

John 8:19

Ephesians 4:18

Ephesians 5:17

1 Peter 2:15

2 Peter 3:8

FORCES OF DARKNESS

Satan and his agents are the forces of darkness that stand to oppose the plan and purpose of God for his children. Satan uses people in the physical, situations and circumstances to bring his evil plans to pass if you are not watchful. Sanballat and Tobiah were used by Satan to hinder the rebuilding of the walls of Jerusalem. However, thank God for Nehemiah since he was in tune with the Holy Spirit and all their devices were brought to complete foolishness. That is the way we should be so their plans will be brought to foolishness. However, if he was not alert, you know what would have happened—the work of God would have been hindered. The thoughts of your heart are his abode—he never departs from your mind if you give him room to come in. Your biggest victory with the thought of your mind is saturating with the word of God. Resists the devil, and above all abstain from all manner of sin so God's name might be glorified. Satan operates every second to get you the child of God destroyed. His mission is to kill and destroy and cause hindrances. God would want you to read your Bible and pray but the devil will try at all cost to distract you from praying and studying your Bible. You have to be alert to be able to recognize when the enemy comes otherwise, you end up not fulfilling the will of God as Satan creeps in to cause afflictions. In some ministries, without question the works of darkness are obvious. We should be aware that believers are in a warfare with the enemy and should not give any occasion for him to come in.

Discuss these scripture verses. What are forces of darkness?
Nehemiah 6:1–16

Daniel 10:11–13

Ephesians 6:12

1 Thessalonians 2:18

FAULTY FOUNDATION

What comparison was made from this particular verse with a foundation?
Luke 6:49

Missions Of Faulty Foundation

As I have kept on saying in this book that faulty foundation is like a debilitating disease. It is terrible and difficult to tell except you have knowledge of it. It can manifest any time in your life if you did not break it through prayers. That is why you see strong ministers of God after a long time in marriage and in ministry, suddenly there is a problem that will end up in separation or in divorce—that is faulty foundation. When you begin to trace how they got married, you will be amazed what happened. Now read carefully, it might not be they sinned. However, it could be who they married was not the right person to help accomplish the calling and ministry God has placed in their lives. God cannot give you his perfect will and later in your journey the person leaves you for somebody else for whatever reason. I have heard some people say—their partner in marriage is doing the work of God too much more than it should be and leaving the family behind. Sometimes I would usually ask, what was your conviction before you married a minister of the gospel? What do you expect to see in your marriage when you marry a minister? Do you expect so many vacation times? That might not happen very much if you truly want to do the work of God effectively. God cannot give you someone who will end your ministry because of his or her selfish desires—that is not God. This is where the perfect will of God and your own will come in. God is perfect and all he does is perfect. However, our will is not perfect hence the wreck we encounter along the line. The devil wants the work of God not to prosper, and he is desperately fighting believers in all areas of their lives—do not give in to the enemy.

To Destroy Your Life And Ruin Your Salvation
What are the missions of the enemy and how can you overcome?
John 10:10

Philippians 2:12

To Render You Fruitless
Mathew 15:1–2a

Mark 11:13–14

Inability To Grasp The Message God Is Relating To You
Discuss these scripture verses.
Romans 8:7, 26

I Corinthians 2:14

NOT BEING WATCHFUL

How can you be watchful?
1 Corinthians 16:13

Ephesians 6:18

Colossians 4:2

1 Peter 5:8

CHAPTER EIGHT

Do You Have To Answer The Call of God?

Besides God there is no other—he is the ultimate in power and his Kingdom cannot be overthrown or defeated. God is the final arbiter—he spoke, it came to pass and he commanded, it stood fast. Fear him that is able to kill and bring back to life. No other can bring back to life except God of power and Righteousness.

GOD ALMIGHTY-THE "REMOTE" CONTROL OF THE ENTIRE UNIVERSE
Deuteronomy 32:39–42

Isaiah 48:12–13

Amos 5:8

Revelation 1:8, 18

(SIMILAR REFERENCES. REVELATION 21:6, 22:3, AND ISAIAH 44:6)

WHY IS GOD IN CHARGE OF ALL?

GOD'S DWELLING PLACE

We generalize heaven as one when we relate or talk about God in heaven. Heaven is of different levels. God our Father lives in heaven and we live on the earth, which is under him. This clearly shows his supremacy over mankind. His eyes see all mankind even without him making a move. No matter how mad and frustrated you might be, you will be the one to look up for help. God does not have to look up because he is already up. This also shows we should be humble before him (2 Chronicles 7:14). Ecclesiastes 5:2 says, "Be not rash with thy mouth, and let not thine heart be hasty to utter anything before God: for God is in heaven, and thou upon earth: therefore let thy word be few." Heaven has three levels: The first, second and third. The first is the sky also known as the firmament that God spoke about in Genesis 1:14, which has clouds that surrounds the entire earth. This is where the birds of the air fly. The second is where the sun, moon, stars are found. Finally, the third heaven is where our Almighty God resides with Jesus Christ our Savior with the holy angels singing and worshipping God around the throne of his mercy seat day and night. In addition, all believers will be here if they do well in the end. Are you ready to go? Strive to go.

FIRST HEAVEN

Discuss these scripture verses.

Deuteronomy 28:12

1 Kings 18:45

Job 4:25

Psalm 147:8–9

Isaiah 55:10

Jeremiah 4:25

Lamentation 4:19

Daniel 7:13–14

Matthew 24:30

Acts 14:17

SECOND HEAVEN
Discuss these scripture verses.
Genesis 1:14–16

Deuteronomy 4:19

Joshua 10:12–13

2 Kings 23:5

Jeremiah 8:2

THIRD HEAVEN
Discuss these scripture verses.
Ecclesiastes 5:2

Psalm 2:1–4

Jeremiah 23:23–24

Mark 16:19

Hebrews 9:24

Ephesians 4:8

1 Timothy 6:16

HIS WISDOM
How is God's wisdom different from that of man?
Job 2:13

Job 9:1–4

Psalm 147:5

Proverbs 2:6

Isaiah 40:28

Isaiah 55:8–11

Micah 6:8

Romans 11:29, 33

James 1:5

THE FUTILITY OF LIFE AND THE WICKEDNESS OF MAN

Discuss these scripture verses.

Genesis 6:5–7

Ecclesiastes 1:1–18

Ecclesiastes 12:8

Jeremiah 17:9

Romans 5:12

1 John 2:15–17

1 John 5:18–19

THE HOLY SPIRIT MAKES THE DIFFERENCE

Discuss theses scripture verses. How can the Holy Spirit cause a change?

Luke 4:1

John 14:26

John 15:26

John 16:8, 13

Romans 8:14, 16, 26

1 Corinthians 2:10–11

THE GIFT OF ETERNITY

What is eternity? Are you looking forward to this?
John 3:15–16, 36

John 5:24

Romans 6:23

CHAPTER NINE

Challenges Ministry Face Generally

PRIDE

Discuss pride with these scripture verses below.
Psalm 10:4

Proverbs 8:13

Proverbs 16:18

Proverbs 29:23

Daniel 5:20

1 John 2:16

FLESH

Discuss these scripture verses. How could your flesh rule you?
Romans 8:1

Romans 8:3–13

Galatians 5:16

What are the works of the flesh from these verses?
Galatians 5:19–21
(1)
(2)
(3)
(4)
(5)
(6)
(7)

(8)

(9)

(10)

(11)

(12)

(13)

(14)

(15)

(16)

(17)

Does any of the above manifest in your life? Flesh is one of the enemies you have in your Christian race. Take this study seriously and ask God to help you overcome by his Spirit. Remember it is a day-to-day battle until Jesus comes. May the Lord help us all in Jesus' name. Amen.

LACK OF LOVE

Discuss these scripture verses.
1 Corinthians 13:1–13

COMPROMISE

How does the scripture address this topic from these verses?
Numbers 15:30–36

Deuteronomy 4:2

Joshua 1:7

Proverbs 30:5–6

Acts 5:1–11

Revelation 2:19–23

RELYING ON PAST ANOINTING

Relying on past anointing is operating in deception. Every child of God needs that in-filling of the Holy Spirit daily to be able to operate effectively on the realm and level of anointing God has given them for their calling. You must have that fresh anointing daily without which you will become a powerless Christian. People might have known you in the past as someone that carries the anointing of God. Are you still whom they think you are? Relying on your previous anointing brings hindrances to the work of God.

Discuss these scriptures.

1 Chronicles 16:11

Isaiah 40:31

Psalm 51:10

Psalm 92:10

Judges 16:19–20

Luke 4:1

Acts 2:4

Acts 4:31

Romans 12:1–3

UNWILLINGNESS TO SERVE
Discuss these scriptures.
Joshua 24:15

Jeremiah 1:5

Romans 12:1

Ephesians 2:1–10

SOME MAY NOT BE GIVEN THE OPPORTUNITY TO SERVE

Consider the leadership in the church and ministry at large. Does our leadership have any influence in the work of God? How?

BEING A STUMBLING BLOCK TO A FELLOW BELIEVER

Discuss these scripture verses.
Leviticus 19:13–15

Isaiah 57:14

Ezekiel 14:3–4

Romans 14:13, 15, 20

2 Corinthians 6:3–4

Galatians 5:13

Colossians 2:8

Revelation 2:14–15

Share your experiences, genuine stories or testimonies. Always remember that testing a fellow believer to find fault with them is not godly. Confess your sins one to another that the blood of Jesus may cleanse you from all unrighteousness. The Lord calls for love among his church Body and John 3:16 should be a constant reminder to us about the heart's desire of our God who does not despise anyone.

CLAIM TO KNOW IT ALL
Proverbs 1:5

1 Corinthians 1:18–19, 25–31

1 Corinthians 3:18–19

1 Corinthians 8:1–2

SPIRIT OF MIRIAM
Numbers 12:1–2, 5–10

What life lessons can you learn from these verses?

Do we have this spirit operating in our churches and ministries today?

James 3:5–6, 8–14

REBELLIOUS SPIRIT OR "BOUNCING BACK SPIRIT"
Discuss these scripture verses.
1 Samuel 15:23

Isaiah 30:1–3

Psalm 78:8

Romans 5:19

LACK OF EFFECTIVE LEADERSHIP
Discuss these scripture verses.
Proverbs 16:12

Proverbs 11:14

Proverbs 29:4, 10

Matthew 15:14

Matthew 23:8–12

IMPROPER DELEGATION OF DUTIES
Discuss these scripture verses.
Exodus 18:13–26

DECEPTION AND CAMOUFLAGE
Discuss these scripture verses.
Jeremiah 17:9–10

Matthew 16:23

2 Corinthians 6:14–18

2 Corinthians 11:14

Ephesians 4:26–27

Colossians 2:8

FINANCES

Discuss these scripture verses.
Deuteronomy 15:10

Proverbs 22:9

Malachi 3:10

Luke 6:38

Luke 12:33

THREAT TO LEAVE THE MINISTRY

Discuss these scripture verses.

Nehemiah 6:9

Ephesians 6:5–9

Colossians 3:22–24

DISCRIMINATION

This is one of heartfelt topics, which is real and true but very hard and sensitive to talk about. Be rest assured, your honest contribution will help others along the line and as well bring blessings in the race.

Do you think this is present and active in our churches and ministries today? YES ___ NO___

How?

Acts 10:34–35

1 Samuel 16:7

Please take some time to discuss these verses of the scriptures. Be able to reflect on what was going on among the brethren in Corinth and relate it to our present-day believers in the church of Christ (1 Corinthians 3:4–11).

Mark 9:38–39, Luke 9:49–50

Galatians 3:28

CHAPTER TEN

How to Enhance a Smooth and Effective Ministry

ALLOW GOD TO BE IN CHARGE

Discuss these scripture verses.
Psalm 37:5

Proverbs 3:5

Psalm 119:133

Proverbs 16:3

Zechariah 4:6

BURY YOUR FLESHLY DESIRES AND AGENDA
Discuss these scripture verses.
Exodus 20:17

Proverbs 18:1

Romans 13:14

Galatians 5:16

Ephesians 4:22

DO NOT BE IN CHARGE OF MINISTRY FINANCES (NEVER)!
Discuss these scripture verses.
1 Timothy 3:1–7

Titus 1:7–11

RESIST ALL MANNER OF DISTRACTIONS
Discuss these scriptures.
Matthew 13:25

1 Corinthians 7:35

James 4:4

BE READY TO ACCEPT YOUR MISTAKES AND MAKE A CHANGE

Discuss these scriptures.
Proverbs 24:16

Isaiah 55:6–7

Revelation 2:5

PRAY CONSISTENTLY

Discuss these scriptures.
Luke 18:1

Ephesians 6:18

1 Thessalonians 5:17

DEDICATION TO THE SERVICES OF GOD

Discuss these scripture verses. How can you present yourself as a living sacrifice to the Lord?

Romans 12:1

1Timothy 4:15

1 Peter 3:15

CONSECRATION LEADS TO HOLINESS

Discuss these scriptures.

Leviticus 11:44

Leviticus 20:7

Ephesians 4:1

Colossians 3:2

Hebrews 12:1

1 Peter 1:15–16

NOTE:

A smooth and effective ministry springs from your intimacy in your personal relationship with the Father, Son and the Holy Spirit. You cannot give what you do not have. As a songwriter rightly puts it, in his presence heaven and earth become one. Then and only then can you likewise say, "Then answered Jesus and said unto them, Verily, verily, I say unto you, The Son can do nothing of himself, but what he seeth the Father do: for what things soever he doeth, these also doeth the Son likewise" (John 5:19). Certainly, a man can receive nothing except it be given him from heaven. Let this attitude guide you as Jesus must increase and we must decrease in our entire endeavors.

CHAPTER ELEVEN

Points Worthy of Note as You Answer
The Call of God For Your Life

YOUR CONVICTION

Discuss these scriptures.
Daniel 3:16–19

Acts 17:11

1 Corinthians 15:58

Philippians 1:6

Hebrews 11:11

TAKE COGNIZANCE OF WOLVES IN SHEEP CLOTHING
Discuss these scriptures.
Acts 20:29

Romans 16:17–27

2 Timothy 4:3–4

BEWARE OF THE UNDECIDED
Discuss these scriptures.
James 1:8

Revelation 3:16

DISCERNMENT SPIRIT FROM GOD—A MUST HAVE
This is one of the must have gifts in our Christian race today. Why?

Discuss these scriptures.
1 Kings 3:9

Philippians 1:9–10

Do you have this gift? If not, you need it urgently because you will never run this race effectively without the discernment spirit manifesting fully in your life. Pray and ask God to send it upon you so you might be effective in your calling.

CHAPTER TWELVE

The Enemies of Your Christian Life

THE WORLD

We live in the world and Jesus said, yet we are not of the world. How does that work? Indeed, we are in the world and everything in the world God created is around us. However, the system of this world is against God. Therefore, if you are of God and the system is against God—is against you too. What do you do? Run for your life or else you will join the system and hate God too. That is why the world is the enemy of your Christian life. The government of God is different from the government of the world system. Your salvation is very expensive so you have to fight this battle to win. If you are not on your guard, you will end up losing your salvation in an attempt to be like the people of this world.

Discuss these scripture verses.

Romans 12:2

James 4:4

1 John 2:15–17

According to 1 John 2:16, what are the characteristics of the world?
(a)
(b)
(c)
How can you be entangled with (a)?

How can you be entangled with (b)?

How can you be entangled with (c)?

In what areas do you find yourself following the patterns of this world in your walk with God? Be honest and sincere to yourself. Your honesty and willingness to change brings your deliverance.

HOW TO OVERCOME THE WORLD
1 Corinthians 6:14–17

1 John 5:3–5

THE FLESH

Flesh can rule you all your life if you are not watchful. The most important thing to understand when it comes to flesh is your motive for doing anything. Your intention matters so much in anything you do. Some people do whatever they choose to do in the house of God just to satisfy their flesh and it is assumed they are doing the work of God. Some are not serving God or Satan but they are serving their own flesh. This is to tell you what the flesh can do to you. That desire to please you and not God is not of God. If you love God you should always seek to please him. If you want to fast, let food alone and when you are done fasting you can eat. If you want to fast and you are struggling between food and fast—the food is your flesh trying to rule you because the body wants food and cannot endure. When you cannot subject that desire and you go ahead to eat, your flesh has taken the upper hand against you instead of the Spirit of God. The flesh continues to fight the spirit but it will be your responsibility not to give up but allow the Spirit of God to take over. That is why these opposers are called your enemies and you face them on a daily basis. This will continue until Jesus comes—not easy but by the grace of God we will overcome.

Discuss these scriptures.
Romans 7:22–23

Romans 8:12–13

Galatians 5:17

1 Timothy 4:1

1 Peter 2:11

HOW TO OVERCOME THE FLESH
Romans 8:1–5

What are the areas you have walked in the flesh instead of walking in the spirit whether deliberately or not? (Remember your motive for doing anything is important).

In your family, in what areas or occasions have you walked in the flesh instead of in the spirit?

In your personal life, in what areas have you walked in the flesh instead of in the spirit when it comes to food, physical possessions and achievements?

In the areas of physical outfit, adornment and beauty, have you ever walked in the flesh instead of in the spirit?

In the things of God—prayers, Bible study, witnessing etc. Have you walked in the flesh instead of in the spirit?

In the church when it comes to church attendance, teaching or helping in any area as an act of service onto God, have you walked in the flesh instead of in the spirit?

How often have you seen a brother or a sister fast approaching your direction and you took a different direction just because you cannot withstand him or her for some reasons best known to you?

How often have you neglected a call, email, text from a sister or a brother because you were mad for something you have not even related to him or her?

Pray that God will help you to walk in the spirit always, so you will not fulfill the desires of your flesh. Pray for every child of God in your family, church and in the world at large for God to have mercy and deliver his people from bondage of flesh in Jesus' name. Amen.

SATAN

Satan is our accuser. He goes about seeking how to destroy us. By the grace of God his plans will not proper. However, we have to follow the example Jesus laid for us to overcome him. He is mean and subtle. He walks in disguise.

Discuss these scriptures.

Ephesians 6:12

2 Timothy 2:26

1 Peter 5:8

1 John 3:8

HOW TO OVERCOME SATAN
James 4:7

Ephesians 6:10–13

Ephesians 6:14–18

According to the Bible verses above, we have ____number of amour of God. What are they? What does each represent in our walk with God today? (1)

REPRESENTS WHAT?

(2)

REPRESENTS WHAT?

(3)

REPRESENTS WHAT?

(4)

REPRESENTS WHAT?

(5)

REPRESENTS WHAT?

(6)

REPRESENTS WHAT?

What are the recommendations in verse 18?

(a)

(b)

Why are they important in our walk with God?

What do you think will happen if we fail to follow them as we run our daily Christian race?

How often are we supposed to put on the armour of God?

How many amour of God can you put on at a time?

Is any of the amour of God more important than the other?

What happens if you put on one and leave the rest? Or none at all?

CHAPTER THIRTEEN

The Gospel We Preach

According to these verses, the gospel we preach are called what?
Matthew 4:23

1 Peter 4:17

Mark 1:1, Galatians 1:7

Ephesians 1:13

2 Corinthians 5:19

Ephesians 6:15

Acts 20:24

1 Timothy 1:11

Revelation 14:6

CHAPTER FOURTEEN

The Enemies of The Gospel of Jesus Christ

THE DEATH OF JESUS CHRIST IS NOT SUFFICIENT FOR THE SALVATION OF MAN

Step-by-step following of laid down rules, procedures and conventions of man will never give salvation to any human being on earth. Faith and the grace of God through Jesus Christ only can give salvation to mankind. It is not by works, effort or your righteousness. Christ sacrificed himself on the cross for our sins so that we might be set free. God did not demand us to sacrifice ourselves for the sin we have committed against him rather he sent his Son who knew no sin for our sakes. He is the only God that does not demand sacrifice but all other gods demand sacrifice from their worshippers. Those gods play games of give and take, and you will be held captive all your life except you repent. The result or effect of law is that you will always remain in bondage—that is the law for you.

Discuss these scriptures.

Romans 3:19–22

Romans 4:4–6

Galatians 2:3–5

Have you tried in your own way to help Jesus by adding to the finished work on the cross?

Are you running your Christian race by your own strength and effort or by the grace of God?

GRACE ____ YOUR EFFORT? ____

Why did you choose your answer above?

HOW DO YOU KNOW YOU ARE WALKING BY THE GRACE OF GOD OR BY YOUR OWN HUMAN EFFORT?

TAKE A TEST-DRIVE

Things have to be done in your own way or there will be problems.

Are you always controlling and giving commands to others?

You will not always follow directions from anyone else in authority except, it is your wish.

You are always right, and every other person is wrong.

You always have a set standard to follow, and if you fail to keep it, you are angry, frustrated, and condemn yourself.

You are always angry and devastated when other people did not meet up with your own standards.

If you answered yes to any of these, you need the grace of God to run this race otherwise, you will be tired and fall by the wayside. Human effort can only go thus far, however, the grace of God endures forever—embrace the grace of God in all you do. Ask God to deliver you from self and pray with all your heart for his grace upon your spirit, soul and body so it might be well with you.

FALSE DOCTRINE

The greatest enemy of the gospel of Jesus Christ is false doctrine. False doctrine is the deceit of Satan to lure people to hell. If you love the LORD you have to obey his commandments. Satan brings counterfeits here and there through people that call themselves ministers of the gospel. Watch out they are all over. Paul had a taste of it hence he marveled with the Galatians for following strange gospel other than the gospel of Christ he brought to them. When people are not walking in the true light of the word of God, they are bound to operate outside the will of God for their lives. The Bible says in John 14:6, "Jesus said unto him, I am the way, the truth, and the life: no man cometh unto the father, but by me." Any doctrine outside the word of God is false. Any addition or subtraction to God's word is false. Anyone twisting God's word to suit his or her evil desires is heading for God's wrath.

Therefore, be alert and follow the standard of the word of God in the true Holy Bible. You have to search the scriptures to find out all you have heard and balance it out with what God said. You cannot believe all spirits. You have to discern to make sure they are of God. There are so many false teachings in the world today. These false teachings and they that teach them are all enemies of the gospel of Jesus Christ and you have to run away from them. Romans 16:17 says, "Now I beseech you, brethren, mark them which cause divisions and offences contrary to the doctrine which ye have learned; and avoid them." They like to argue about the word of God and the whole point of the argument is to convince you to believe in their lies. Do not go close rather run for them. Some of them willingly deceive people hence that is their job from their father Satan. Because they are doing it to get people, they are desperate to argue until you give up. That is why you have to know what God said in his word. Jesus gave his warning in Matthew 24:11, "And many false prophets shall rise, and and shall deceive many."

Discuss these scriptures.
Matthew 7:15–16

Matthew 15:9

Colossians 2:8

1 Timothy 4:1

2 Timothy 4:3–4

1 Peter 2:1–3

2 John 1:7

How can I be sure I do not believe in false doctrine? How can I verify what I believe?

John 8:32

John 14:6

2 Timothy 2:15

Ephesians 4:14

Hebrews 13:9

DENYING THE HUMANITY OF JESUS CHRIST

Jesus is both God and man—mystery. God is mystery, and all his works are mysterious. His Son Jesus Christ coming to die for sinners is also mysterious. In the normal sense, he did not have to die for sins he did not commit. However, God made him to do so because of his love for mankind. That love we do not even deserve to have. Man was in a miserable state—eternal death because of sin. In addition, nothing else could have saved man from such judgment than the blood of Jesus. There are many mystical things about God that no matter what you try to understand them you will not instead you go insane trying to understand why God did what he did. He is God, and his understanding is beyond mankind. Jesus is God who came in human form to earth—again mystery. Any doctrine that denies Jesus as the Son of God who came in the flesh is false. Again, study to show yourself approved. There are many references in the Bible that show who he is and all his accounts. Do not let any man deceive you.

Discuss these scriptures.

John 2:19–21

John 20:19–20

Luke 24:39–40

Jesus ate physical food (Matthew 26:17, 19-21, 23, 26).

COMMENTS:

He was overwhelmed with situations and circumstances around him as we do today (Matthew 26:38–46).

COMMENTS:

He had flesh, blood and water in his body (John 19:34).

COMMENTS:

He died on the cross (John 19:30).

COMMENTS:

He was buried (John 19:38–42).

He was raised from the grave by the power of God Almighty (John 20:1–13).

Jesus manifested himself to Mary and to his disciples (John 20:14–31 John 21:1–14).

COMMENTS:

His resurrection is the victory believers have to proclaim the gospel (Revelation 1:18, 2 Corinthians 15:14).

COMMENTS:

DENYING THE SUPREMACY OF JESUS CHRIST

Jesus defeated the power of grave hence it could not hold him back. Revelation 1:18 says, "I am he that liveth, and was dead; and, behold, I am alive for evermore, Amen; and have the keys of hell and of death." Our victory is based on the ability of Jesus to rise from the grave on the third day by the power of the Most High God. Brethren this is our boldness before principalities and power, false religion, false doctrine and teaching and all Satanic devices to wipe away the work of God on the cross through Christ Jesus.

From the following verses, who is the person of Jesus Christ?
Colossians 1:15

Colossians 1:16

Colossians 1:17

Colossians 1:18

Colossians 1:19

Colossians 1:20

Do you believe the Bible to be the written word of God?   Yes __ No __

Do you believe Colossians 1:15–20 as in above?   Yes__ No __

Do you also believe that Jesus Christ is supreme over every created thing both visible and invisible?

COMMENTS:

NOTE:

If you have been taught anything contrary to the above scripture verses about the supremacy of Jesus Christ that is a false Doctrine.

CHAPTER FIFTEEN

I Am Deeply Concerned With "Christianity" in Our World Today

In your own words, how would you explain or describe what is going on in our Christian world today?

Who is a true Christian?

Would you consider yourself a true Christian? Why?

If Jesus were to return now are you ready to go with him?

Do you feel comfortable to serve God in truth and in spirit in the house God? Why your answer?

Based on your experience and dealings with God, do you think that anyone who calls himself or herself a Christian is a real Christian? Why?

Have you had any encounter with some people that call themselves Christians and later you found out the truth is far from them?

Do you have any old man in you that needed to be destroyed? Explain.

What are your plans to make our Christian walk with God encouraging for one another?

Take sometime to write down the prayer points and things you want to see happen in the house of God so our burden may be lighter and easier and that men may serve God out of a true spirit. Your prayers will cause a change. Pray those until you feel the burden lifted off your shoulders.

ii) WHAT THE CHURCH OF JESUS CHRIST "IS NOT"

"Not forsaking the assembling of ourselves together, as the manner of some is; but exhorting one another: and so much the more, as ye see the day approaching" (Hebrews 10:2).

The purpose of God for encouraging his children to gather is to edify one another not to entertain one another. The body of Christ has lost the original will and plan of God for coming together just in an attempt to satisfy their flesh. A preacher does not preach the word of God for men to approve him or her rather preaches without addition or subtraction to the word. He or she should not present the word of God as though it were a fun idea to amuse people. In other words, approaching the word of God as a comedy is deceit of the enemy. Paul the apostle in each of his preaching preached the word as it is. Men might approve you but be rest assured that God is a righteous judge, who will judge every individual accordingly. The Bible says in 2 Corinthians 10:18, "For not he that commendeth himself is approved, but whom the Lord commendeth."

THE CHURCH IS NOT AN ENTERTAINMENT THEATER

In what ways has the church seem to become an entertainment theater?

What effect has this on the word of God?

How does this affect the ministers of the gospel?

How about in the body of Christ, what effect has it made?

Are you satisfied with this transition?

How can this be resolved?

THE CHURCH IS NOT A SOCIAL GATHERING

Do you agree the house of God is not a social gathering rather a dwelling place of the Holy Spirit? Yes __ No __Why? (Comment on the following below.)

The preacher preaching the word of God?

The congregation receiving the message or supposedly the word of God.

Praise and worship, including special dances and sounds of instruments, etc.

THE CHURCH IS NOT MADE UP OF SPECTATORS RATHER SOLDIERS

In the house of God, do you consider yourself a soldier or a spectator? *Give the answer to yourself.*

Are you doing the work of God? Have you considered working in his vineyard? *Give the answers to yourself.*

PRAYER POINTS FOR ALL SPECTATORS IN THE HOUSE OF GOD

All the pew warmers today we turn them into soldiers of Christ in Jesus' name. Amen.

Those the enemy has deceived not to see the need to work for God, today we pray for the zeal and fire of God in their lives, so they will not contain it until they have surrendered onto him in Jesus' name. Amen.

We come against you Satan. All you powers of darkness standing against our brethren from seeing the need to serve God with all their hearts, today we break your strongholds in their lives and we set them free in Jesus' name. Amen.

Thank you Jesus for answering and thank you for setting them free in Jesus' name. Amen.

THE CHURCH IS NOT ABOUT YOU

Do you agree that the church or ministry is not about any individual but about Christ? Yes __ No__

Give reasons for your answers as touching these areas:

Personal Achievements: wealth, possessions, inheritance, beauty, eloquence, etc.

COMMENTS:

THE CHURCH IS NOT A PERSONAL PROPERTY

How can ministers or those in authority and in charge of God's work personalize the work of God?

What are the effects of personalizing God's work?

Thanks for all your attempts. I would like to add to your answers. (1) When someone who is financially active leaves the church, the people in charge might not be very pleased hence walking in the flesh which sometimes in the physical might be difficult to notice. Are these happening today in the house of God? One hundred percent yes. (2) They will continue to go deeper in their flesh as they seek different avenues to propel others to walk with them to accomplish their own desires. (3) They operate and walk in disguise employing their fleshly power to praise others to gain approval of men (4) They are more interested in larger ministry, population and finances than the salvation of men. (5) They never give anyone who disagrees with

144

their ideas an opportunity to serve under their leadership. The result of this is that God's work will not function smoothly and effectively. That is why you see some ministers struggling in their ministries beyond normal—walking in flesh. God's work is not supposed to be based on personal decisions rather by the Spirit of God. Flesh is taking over the body of Christ. What can you do then? Pray for those in authority because some of them are just deceivers—do not be deceived. In God's ministry, there should not be any strife. God calls, commissions and continues to use you based on your obedience and submission to him, as he wants you to grow. When you are in a place, and he feels there is a need to go into higher level, he does that without consulting anybody. All he needs from you is obedience. So when God has called somebody for a different mission, it should not be strife instead it should be of joy and thanksgiving to God. However, when you take Gods work to be your personal property and things fail to go the way you wanted there will be confusion and you will begin to find fault with people around you. Give God a chance to do things the way he wants, and you shall be free and above all—you will have peace of mind.

Discuss these scriptures.

Galatians 5:16–21

Jude 1:16

HOW TO OVERCOME

Galatians 5:22–24

GALATIANS 5:24 (IMPORTANT)

PRAYER POINTS

Pray for all churches and ministries at large for God to have mercy upon all the leaders.

Pray that God will visit and touch them so they will begin to obey the word of God they preach daily. (The word of God is for everybody both to the preacher and to the listener or even the reader).

Pray that God will pour down his Spirit upon the leaders that they will operate by the Spirit of God rather than in their own flesh.

Bind the spirit of the last days so it will be far from every true child of God in Jesus' name. Amen.

Pray that God will not allow any of his own to perish rather that he will chasten them according to his will and purpose concerning them until they surrender onto him.

Now, you may pray for anything else you perceive going on among the leaders.

THE CHURCH IS NOT A BUSINESS ENTERPRISE
Romans 16:18

Philippians 3:18–19

In your own words, explain how the work of God has been turned into a business enterprise.

THE CHURCH IS NOT A SECRET GROUP

Who are the believers and what is the purpose for coming together?
1 Corinthians 12:27

Ephesians 2:22–23

Colossians 1:18

Hebrews 4:9

Hebrews 10:24–25

1 Corinthians 3:11

What are your works in the body of Christ?

According to the grace of God which is given unto me, as a wise masterbuilder, I have laid the foundation, and another buildeth thereon. But let every man take heed how he buildeth there upon

(1 Corinthians 3:10).

THE DECLARATION OF JESUS CHRIST ON HIS CHURCH (ALL BELIEVERS)
Matthew 16:16–17

Matthew 16:18–19

THE CHURCH IS NOT MEANT TO CONFORM TO THIS EARTHLY SYSTEM
Romans 12:1–2

2 Corinthians 6:14–18

What is worldliness?

Can a born again Christian be worldly? Yes __ No__

How can a believer conform to the patterns of this world?

Is it godly for a believer to conform to the patterns of this world? Yes __ No __
Explain the reason for your answer above.

THIS IS WHAT THE BIBLE SAYS:
John 15:18

John 17:14

James 1:27

James 4:4

1 John 2:15

Should believers look haggard wearing worn-out or one outfit every time then? Yes __ No __ Explain.

THIS IS WHAT THE BIBLE SAYS:
1 Timothy 2:9

1 Peter 3:3–4

Should we continue to chase after the latest style and fashion of physical outfits, though we appear modest? Alternatively, with any other earthly possessions not limited to cars, aircraft, houses, etc. Yes __ No __

Why did you choose your answer above?

THIS IS WHAT THE BIBLE SAYS:
2 Kings 5:20–27

From these verses what are the effects of covetousness? (Working hard at all cost to get what your flesh wants).

What sin did Gehazi commit in verse 22, 25 joint with his covetousness?

What lesson can we learn from the act of Gehazi?

What is his reward for his act in verse 27?

Luke 12:15

Hebrews 13:5

THE CHURCH IS NOT A GROUND FOR IMITATION

If God has called you into the ministry, he is also able to direct you on what to do even in times of difficulties. God cannot call you and later tell you oh! My daughter or my son you are on your own—that is impossible. The problem is that you have lost contact with him by doing things your own way. God wants you to be original so you might be able to bring out that which he has planted inside of you but when you go around mirroring others, you might end up struggling more than normal. However, recharge by coming to the Lord so you will begin to tap from his source of power and your ministry and calling will rekindle again with fire from the throne of God. Go and do not allow the enemy to cheat you for he is a traditional liar. You are well able to serve God in truth and in righteousness by the power of Jesus.

Discuss these scriptures.

Psalm 34:10

Psalm 50:15

Proverbs 3:5

Isaiah 55:6

Jeremiah 29:3

Jeremiah 33:3

James 1:5–6

THE CHURCH IS NOT A PLACE FOR COMPETITION

Discuss these scriptures
1 Corinthians 3:3–8

1 Corinthians 4:20

Zechariah 4:6

THE CHURCH IS NOT A PLACE YOU MOMENTARILY COME TO FEEL GOOD

Discuss these scriptures.
Psalms 18:30

Psalm 100:5

Psalm 138:8

Proverbs 10:22

THE CHURCH IS NOT A PLACE FOR FOOD AND DRINK ONLY
Discuss these scriptures.
Deuteronomy 8:3

Matthew 4:4

Romans 14:17

THE CHURCH IS NOT A PLACE OF COMPROMISE
Discuss these scriptures.
Acts 10:34–35

Revelation 22:18:19

THE CHURCH IS NOT A POLITICAL FORUM
Discuss these scriptures.
1 Corinthians 1:19–20

1 Corinthians 3:19

CHAPTER SIXTEEN

Strategies of Satan to Entangle and Deceive Many in These Perilous Times (Beware)!

THE DECEIT OF SATAN IN THE HOUSE OF GOD

How? Discuss these scriptures and give your own instances.
Matthew 7:15–16

Acts 13:10

2 Corinthians 11:12–15

2 Peter 2:1–3

2 Thessalonians 2:3–4

MAXIMUM MANIFESTATIONS OF WORKS OF THE FLESH

Explain in your own way what you think this means. Then discuss these scripture verses.

Galatians 5:19–21

SPIRIT OF REBELLION OR "BOUNCING BACK SPIRIT"

Discuss these scriptures.

Psalm 78:8

Isaiah 30:1

CROWD FOLLOWERS

There are some today who claim to know Jesus but the truth is far from them. They started going to church through an invitation and never had any personal touch nor received Christ yet claim to be Christian. During Christmas, people celebrate the birth of Jesus yet they have no idea who he is or the main reason for his birth. God have mercy. In the Bible, Jesus asked his disciples questions concerning who people think he is, and finally, he redirected the question to them. Find out more from these verses.

Matthew 16:13–16 (Explain).

Do you know Jesus? YES __ NO __ Are you born again? YES __ NO __

Share how you were saved and your experience, how it all happened.

It is difficult to find out if a person is saved or not especially during the communal gathering and worship to exalt the name of God in the sanctuary, Bible study group or any other Christian gathering. It would take a courageous person to own up to say he or she is but a churchgoer rather everybody claims to be born again and right with God in such forum and atmosphere. Thus, no one has the right to judge any man and God has not permitted any to judge his fellow but by their fruits, you shall know them. It might not be instantly; however, the fruit they bear will testify against them. One can only hide but for a while.

Please pray for those who have not received Jesus Christ as their Lord and personal Savior in your midst if any. Furthermore, pray for the church body and for those who have no clue about Jesus though in church. Pray for a personal touch of the Lord upon them and their lives will never remain the same in Jesus' name. Amen.

THERE IS NO GOD
Discuss these scriptures.
Psalm 14:1

Psalm 53:1

LOSS OF INTEREST AND ZEAL IN THE THINGS OF GOD
Romans 12:11–12

Revelation 2:4–5

SELF-SEEKERS INSTEAD OF GOD
Discuss these scriptures.
Matthew 23:5

John 5:44

Romans 2:8

1 Timothy 3:3

2 Timothy 3:2

LOVERS OF MONEY MORE THAN THE WORK OF GOD
Discuss these scriptures.
1 Timothy 6:10

Hebrews 13:5

Matthew 6:24

Luke 16:13–15

HATERS OF THE GOSPEL
Have you ever tried to witness to someone, and he or she would not listen to the gospel? Share your experience. (Pray for such people)

Discuss these scriptures.
Romans 1:16, 30

Amos 5:10

IGNORANT OF THE TRUTH

With reference to these scripture verses, what is truth?
John 8:32

John 14:6

John 17:17

How can someone become ignorant of the truth from these scripture passages?
Hosea 4:6

Ephesians 4:18

BUSY TWENTY-FOUR HOURS—NO TIME FOR GOD

Discuss these scriptures.
2 Thessalonians 3:11

1 Timothy 5:12–12

MIRACLE SEEKERS
Discuss these scriptures.
Matthew 12:39

1 Corinthians 1:22

FEAR ACCOMPANIED BY WORRIES
Discuss these scriptures
Matthew 6:25

Matthew 11:28–30

Philippians 4:6–7

1 Peter 5:7

1 John 4:18

CHAPTER SEVENTEEN

Things That Cannot Take You to Heaven

LIVING IN SECRET SIN: PROVERBS 28:13

How can a believer live in secret sin?

PROFESSIONAL FAULT DETECTOR: MATTHEW 7:1–5

Explain by giving instances of a situation where someone paid attention to every detail of someone else's fault.

What was the result?

BEING A PRO IN THE THINGS OF GOD: 1 CORINTHIANS 10:12

BEING RELIGIOUS: JAMES 1:27, 2 TIMOTHY 3:5

SELF-RIGHTEOUSNESS: ISAIAH 64:6, MATTHEW 6:1, GALATIANS 2:20–21

From the verses above, how can someone operate in self-righteousness?

Can someone who is operating in self-righteousness be saved and have eternal life? Yes __or No __

Explain why you chose your answer above?

Romans 4:4–5

Romans 8:8

.

Romans 10:1–11

Romans 11:6

KEEPING THE TEN COMMANDMENTS: LIST THE TEN COMMANDMENTS FROM EXODUS CHAPTER 20

(1)

(2)

(3)

(4)

(5)

(6)

(7)

(8)

(9)

(10)

Is it possible for man to keep the Ten Commandments judiciously without defaulting in any? Yes ___No ___ why?

Explain these scriptures.
Romans 8:8

Romans 3:19–27

For any man who chooses to operate under the law must keep all without defaulting in any. If you keep one and leave the rest, that will be a problem because when you default in one you have defaulted in all. Why trying to keep the law when the grace of God is available? Does it mean we should continue sinning for more grace? God forbid. We are saved by grace not by our own works.

SOCIAL STATUS AND EARTHLY POSSESSIONS: LUKE 12:15
Explain.

READING THE BIBLE EVERY DAY: 2 CORINTHIANS 3:6
Explain.

GOING TO CHURCH OR CHURCH ACTIVITIES REGULARLY
Is it possible for someone to attend church or church activities regularly and yet far from Jesus? Explain.

Why do you think some go to church or church activities regularly yet the truth is not in them?

Discuss this scripture verse. 2 Timothy 3:5

OBSERVATION OF DAYS, TIMES AND SEASONS: AMOS 5:21, ISAIAH 1:11–14
Explain.

FASHION: 1 TIMOTHY 2:9, 1 PETER 3:3–4
Explain.

HUMAN WISDOM: 1 CORINTHIANS 2:13, 1 CORINTHIANS 3:19, PROVERBS 3:13
Explain.

PUTTING YOUR TRUST IN MAN: PSALM 146:3, ISAIAH 2:22
Explain.

USING MINISTERS OF THE GOSPEL AS A STANDARD INSTEAD OF GOD'S WORD: MATTHEW 19:26, ROMANS 5:12, GALATIANS 1:10

Explain.

IGNORANCE: 1 THESSALONIANS 4:13, 2 PETER 3:5

Explain.

HIDING FROM THE TRUTH: MARK 4:2, 2 JOHN 1:7, JUDE 1:6–7

Explain.

MEN PLEASERS: GALATIANS 1:10, EPHESIANS 6:6, COLOSSIANS 3:22

Explain.

SITTING ON THE FENCE: JAMES 1:8, REVELATION 3:15–16
Explain.

SELF-CONDEMNATION: ROMANS 8:1, TITUS 3:11, 1 JOHN 3:19–24
Explain.

IMPROPER ARGUMENTS OF GOD'S WORD AND THE PERSON OF JESUS: 2 TIMOTHY 2:14, 23, TITUS 3:9
Explain.

LEADING THE LARGEST MINISTRY AND PERFORMING THE GREATEST MIRACLES: 1 SAMUEL 2:9, ECCLESIASTES 9:11, ZECHARIAH 4:6
Explain.

FOLLOWING THE DOCTRINES OF MEN: MATTHEW 7:15, MATTHEW 15:9, COLOSSIANS 2:8, 2 TIMOTHY 4:1

Explain.

NOTES

NOTES